Original title:
Shifting Skies

Copyright © 2024 Creative Arts Management OÜ
All rights reserved.

Author: Clara Whitfield
ISBN HARDBACK: 978-9916-90-726-9
ISBN PAPERBACK: 978-9916-90-727-6

Ebb and Flow Above

Clouds drift softly in the sky,
Their shadows dance as they pass by.
Waves crash gently on the shore,
Nature's rhythm, forevermore.

Moonlight glimmers on the sea,
Whispers of the night set free.
Stars align and guide the tide,
In this vast world, we confide.

Echoes from the Firmament

In the silence, secrets dwell,
Stories ancient, hard to tell.
Voices carried through the night,
Softly fading, out of sight.

Constellations weave their lore,
Mapping dreams from times of yore.
Each twinkle sings a distant tune,
Echoes bright beneath the moon.

Mirage in the Midday Sun

Heat waves shimmer on the ground,
Illusions dance without a sound.
Sandy deserts stretch afar,
Hiding treasures like a star.

Cacti stand with arms out wide,
Guardians of this sun-baked ride.
In the stillness, secrets bloom,
Life persists amidst the gloom.

Journeys in the Ethereal

Beneath the stars, we take our flight,
Chasing dreams through endless night.
Each heartbeat echoes, softly heard,
In silent realms, where souls are stirred.

Winds of time whisper our names,
Guiding us through cosmic games.
Together we will dare to roam,
In the vastness, we find home.

The Flickering Firmament

Stars whisper secrets, soft and bright,
In the velvet sky, they dance at night.
A cosmic ballet, timeless and grand,
Wonders of the universe, gently planned.

Clouds drift slowly, shadows in tow,
Moonlight glimmers on rivers below.
Constellations tell stories old,
In every twinkle, a dream unfolds.

The north wind carries celestial tunes,
While comets glide like silver spoons.
A tapestry woven with silver thread,
Awakening hopes, where dreams are fed.

From dusk till dawn, the firmament glows,
In every heart, a yearning flows.
In this vast expanse, we find our place,
Lost in the beauty of time and space.

Compositions in Flux

Life's melody shifts with each passing day,
A symphony woven in varying sway.
Notes clash and merge, creating a song,
In the chaos of rhythm, we find where we belong.

Moments hang like fragile glass,
Reflecting a future, letting the past pass.
Each breath a stanza, each heartbeat a beat,
In the dance of existence, we move to the heat.

Seasons in colors, from bloom to decay,
The harmony shifts in a delicate play.
With whispers of change that beckon and call,
We rise and we stumble, but learn through it all.

Through trials and laughter, we journey along,
In the fabric of life, we compose our own song.
A tapestry merging both joy and strife,
In this canvas of moments, we paint our life.

Dance of the Wandering Clouds

In the vast embrace of blue skies,
Soft whispers drift and slowly rise.
Tufts of white in a graceful waltz,
Painting dreams where the heart exalts.

They sway and twirl, a silent song,
Floating gently, where they belong.
Moments of magic, fleeting and grand,
A ballet performed by nature's hand.

The sun pirouettes, casting its glow,
Fleeting shadows begin to flow.
With each turn, the skies rearrange,
In the dance of the wandering, sweet change.

As daylight fades and stars emerge,
The clouds dissolve in the evening surge.
With every dusk, they're sure to return,
In the dance of the wandering, we learn.

The Colors of Change

Leaves whisper tales of the autumn's breeze,
Painting the ground with vibrant ease.
Golds and reds in a crocus field,
Nature's canvas, a beauty revealed.

The sunsets cast their warm embrace,
Illuminating twilight with radiant grace.
Shadows stretch as colors merge,
In the quiet, all hearts surge.

Springtime blooms, a fragrant delight,
Colors awaken, dispelling the night.
Each petal tells a story anew,
Of hope, of life, and love born true.

From winter's chill to summer's reign,
The cycle spins, and we remain.
In every hue, a lesson to share,
The colors of change, the world laid bare.

Ephemeral Landscapes Above

The sky unfolds like a fleeting dream,
Waves of clouds in a sunlit beam.
Shapes that morph in a dance divine,
Ephemeral glimpses, a world benign.

Mountains of vapor, rolling like sea,
Whispering secrets of what used to be.
In twilight's hour, they flicker and fade,
Moments of beauty, never long stayed.

Stars peek through in the deep of night,
Painting the dark with a silvery light.
Each twinkle a memory, a lost refrain,
In ephemeral landscapes, we long for the same.

As dawn approaches, they softly wane,
Shimmering echoes of joy and pain.
Though fleeting, their wonder forever stays,
Ephemeral landscapes in twilight's gaze.

When Daybreak Meets Twilight

Morning whispers as night withdraws,
Sun stretching wide, embracing its cause.
Birds awaken, with songs of delight,
A fresh start blooms with soft morning light.

Shadows linger, reluctant to fade,
In the embrace of the new day's parade.
Colors spill like a painter's brush,
As nature dances in a tranquil hush.

When twilight falls, a gentle sigh,
Stars peek out in the velvet sky.
The world slows down in the evening's gold,
As stories of daybreak softly unfold.

In this moment where light and dark meet,
Whispers of time held in silence sweet.
Together they weave a tapestry bright,
When daybreak meets twilight, hearts take flight.

Reflections of Tomorrow

In the stillness of dawn,
Dreams weave through the light.
Each step a whisper,
Echoes of what's in sight.

Tomorrow's canvas awaits,
Colors blend and collide.
Hope dances on edges,
Time's gentle tide.

Thoughts drift like blossoms,
Floating on morning air.
In quiet contemplation,
Future laid bare.

In the heart of silence,
Possibilities bloom.
Every heartbeat whispers,
Secrets in the gloom.

The Alchemy of Sun and Moon

Where day kisses night,
Shadows begin to play.
Golden rays melt softly,
Chasing gray away.

The sun's warm embrace,
A dance of fire and breeze.
While moonlight wraps gently,
In stories that please.

Stars twinkle like secrets,
In the velvet above.
Nature hums a sweet tune,
Of harmony and love.

In this sacred balance,
Two forces intertwine.
A journey eternal,
Through space, they align.

Passage of the Ether

In the canvas of blue,
Clouds drift like a dream.
Time flows in silence,
Life's intricate seam.

Whispers of the cosmos,
Call out through the night.
The stars are our guide,
In gentle starlight.

Journey through the void,
Where darkness meets the glow.
Each heartbeat a promise,
Of what we may know.

Threads of connection,
Knit us, hand in hand.
In the passage of ether,
Together we stand.

Aether's Embrace

In the twilight's embrace,
Soft breaths intertwine.
Nature hums a lullaby,
With the stars that shine.

Whispers through the trees,
Carried on the breeze.
Aether's gentle touch,
Brings comfort and ease.

Through the realms we wander,
Exploring skies above.
In the cradle of night,
We find peace and love.

In the stillness of dreams,
Hope's melody plays.
A tapestry of light,
In aether's warm gaze.

Pulse of the Universe

In the depths of night, stars collide,
Rhythms of cosmos, vast and wide.
Galaxies dance, a cosmic show,
Whispers of time in an endless flow.

Planets spin in silent grace,
Echoes of ancient, timeless space.
Sprinkled stardust, dreams take flight,
Painting the canvas of endless night.

Each heartbeat a light, a cosmic sign,
Connecting the threads of the divine.
In every pulse, the universe sings,
Life's fleeting moments, infinite things.

Through dark and light, we shall roam,
In the universe's heart, we find our home.
Boundless echoes that never cease,
In the pulse of existence, we find peace.

Light's Ephemeral Journey

A beam breaks through the morning haze,
Glistening dew in a soft blaze.
Every flicker, a fleeting grace,
Moments captured in time's embrace.

Rays of gold on the edges gleam,
Whispers of hope in a soft dream.
Chasing shadows, light dances free,
Tracing paths through eternity.

Yet even stars, they fade away,
Telling stories of yesterday.
In every glow, a tale begun,
Fleeting sparks of the setting sun.

Hold tight to light, though it may wane,
In its warmth, there's joy, there's pain.
A journey brief, but brightly shone,
In light's embrace, we're never alone.

Unraveling Threads

Tapestry woven with colors bright,
Each thread whispers tales of light.
Knots of joy, stitches of pain,
In every weave, life's sweet refrain.

Pull one thread, and see it flow,
Connections made, hearts aglow.
Fragile fibers that intertwine,
In the fabric of time, we define.

Frayed edges tell of battles won,
Silent stories of what was spun.
Each unraveling brings forth new,
An art of life in every hue.

Together we stitch, together we tear,
Creating beauty, embracing despair.
In this weaving, we find our fate,
Unraveling threads, we contemplate.

The Enigma of Ephemerality

Petals fall in the gentle breeze,
Whispers of time, delicate tease.
Moments vanish with the dawn,
In their passing, the heart is drawn.

Fleeting shadows, the sun's decline,
Memories linger, yet intertwined.
Nature's dance in a soft embrace,
In the ephemeral, we find our place.

Life unfolds in a breath's short span,
Every heartbeat, a fleeting plan.
In the mystery lies the grace,
A gentle touch we can't replace.

Cherish the now, for it will fade,
In the web of life, we are laid.
Embrace the moment, let it be,
In the enigma, we are set free.

Reflections in the Liquid Sky

The sky cascades with hues of blue,
Mirroring dreams, both old and new.
Rippling whispers of gentle grace,
In liquid realms, we find our place.

Clouds dance lightly on the breeze,
Cradling secrets with such ease.
Sunsets bleed in colors bright,
As day surrenders to the night.

Each star reflects a tale untold,
In this vast canvas, dreams unfold.
Rippling waters and skies collide,
In liquid depths, we confide.

The moon hangs low, a silver kite,
Guiding hearts through velvet night.
In stillness, we gather our fears,
Beneath the sky, we shed our tears.

Secrets Beneath a Transient Canopy

Leaves whisper softly in the breeze,
Tales of time lost in the trees.
Underneath the boughs, shadows play,
Secrets linger as light fades away.

Beneath the canopy, hearts collide,
In nature's arms, we're drawn inside.
Branches intertwine like souls that yearn,
In fleeting moments, we discern.

Rustling roots cradle ancient lore,
Tapping into the earth's core.
Life ebbs and flows in rhythmic dance,
In the quiet, we take a chance.

Stars peek through in scattered light,
Guiding our way through the night.
Each leaf a story, each gust a sigh,
Under this canopy, we learn to fly.

The Flicker of Farewell Stars

In twilight's grasp, the stars ignite,
Flickering gently, a soft goodbye.
Whispers of cosmos fill the air,
As night unfolds its velvet layer.

Each twinkle holds a memory dear,
Of wanderers lost, and dreams unclear.
In distant realms, their light transcends,
The flicker fades, but never ends.

A glance above can spark a thought,
Of battles fought and love that's sought.
Silent wishes on stardust trails,
Through cosmic seas, our spirit sails.

As dawn approaches, shadows part,
The stars may fade, but not the heart.
In every flicker, echoes soar,
Farewell stars, we'll seek you more.

Chronicles of an Altered Firmament

In skies where colors twist and blend,
New tales of wonder softly send.
The firmament breathes, shifts, and sways,
In altered forms, it lays its praise.

Clouds morph shapes, a painter's dream,
Sketching stories that brightly gleam.
Here, the sun and moon unite,
In a dance of day and night.

Stars etch paths across the dark,
Guiding souls to find their spark.
In constellations, whispers gleam,
Chronicled hopes in a celestial stream.

Under this dome, we weave our fates,
In realms where destiny awaits.
With every glance, we find our truth,
In the firmament's endless youth.

Chasing the Tides of Time

The ocean whispers, tales untold,
As waves collide, both fierce and bold.
Chasing moments, we find our way,
Through sands of hours, night turns to day.

Each fleeting second, it dances by,
Like shadows cast from a sunlit sky.
We race the currents, heartbeats align,
In the rhythm of life, we're free, divine.

Beneath the Starlit Canopy

In twilight's grasp, the world fades slow,
Beneath the stars, where dreams can grow.
A soft breeze whispers, secrets sweet,
Guiding the wanderers, hearts that beat.

Constellations shimmer, stories weave,
Each twinkle a promise, if we believe.
Under the blanket of night we unite,
Finding our path in the soft, gentle light.

Symphony of the Clouds

Clouds gather high, in hues of grey,
A symphony plays as the skies sway.
Raindrops fall like notes from afar,
Each drop a reminder, we're never far.

The thunder rumbles, a powerful song,
In the dance of the storm, we all belong.
Nature's orchestra, wild and free,
A melody heard by you and me.

Shadows in the Glow

Where light flickers, shadows creep,
In corners dark, secrets sleep.
The glow reveals what lies within,
A tapestry woven, where tales begin.

Figures dance in the amber light,
Echoes of laughter, a soft delight.
In the twilight hour, we come alive,
With shadows beside us, together we thrive.

The Unraveling Canvas

Colors bleed and swirl away,
Brushstrokes blend like night and day.
Dreams spill forth in vibrant streams,
Life's creation births new themes.

Fragments torn from every hue,
Memories lost, yet somehow true.
Heartbeats echo on the page,
Art and time both share a stage.

Minds engage with every shade,
In silence, now our fears evade.
The canvas speaks without a sound,
In its embrace, new worlds are found.

A masterpiece of wish and woe,
In the chaos, still we grow.
With every stroke, we redefine,
The story's end, a tangled line.

Flight of the Spirits

Whispers soar on gentle breeze,
Echoes dance among the trees.
Guided by the stars' soft glow,
Spirits weave where wild winds blow.

Through the night, they glide and twirl,
In a dreamlike, endless whirl.
Each flutter whispers tales untold,
Of longing hearts, both brave and bold.

In the moonlight's tender grace,
They embark from sacred place.
Infinity in every flight,
Navigating through the night.

Onward they chase the dawn's first light,
Leaving traces, pure delight.
Together bound, yet free they roam,
In the sky, they find their home.

Alchemy of the Atmosphere

Air thickens with a golden hue,
Sunset paints a world anew.
Harvest moons and twilight glow,
Nature's breath begins to flow.

Sorcery in the softest breeze,
Changing heartbeats, bending knees.
Feel the weight, the pulse, the sigh,
Magic dwells in the open sky.

Every cloud, a dream unfold,
Whispers of the tales once told.
Storms brew deep, yet peace shall reign,
In their calm, we feel no pain.

Moments caught in fleeting air,
A tapestry of joy and care.
Here within this mystic sphere,
All is woven, all is clear.

Beyond the Veil of Blue

Horizon stretches, vast and wide,
Secrets wait where tides abide.
Beyond the veil, the unknown calls,
In whispers soft, the mystery falls.

Waves of thought rise, ebb, and flow,
Dancing dreams beneath the glow.
Journey forth through cosmic streams,
Into the realm of silent dreams.

Stars align, they sing a tune,
Guiding souls beneath the moon.
Each moment lives in shades of light,
Turning shadows into sight.

Embrace the vastness, lose your fear,
For magic lives when you draw near.
Beyond the blue, where wonders lie,
In the depths, our spirits fly.

Where Dreams Touch the Zenith

In the stillness of the night,
Whispers dance with silver light.
Stars align, a cosmic play,
While dreams unfold in soft array.

Eyes closed tight, the heart takes flight,
Over mountains, into night.
Guided by the moon's embrace,
Journeying to a sacred space.

Each heartbeat, a gentle sigh,
Melodies from worlds up high.
In silence, find the hidden truth,
Where youth meets the eternal youth.

And when the dawn begins to break,
New horizons softly wake.
In the glow, let visions blend,
For every dream has no end.

Embrace of Twilight's Kiss

As day surrenders to the night,
Shadows weave a dance of light.
The horizon blushes deep,
While memories around us creep.

Crickets sing their evening song,
In the twilight, we belong.
Lost in hues of purple skies,
Every moment softly flies.

In the stillness, hearts will meet,
Gentle whispers, love's heartbeat.
Wrapped in warmth, we find our way,
Balancing the dusk and day.

With each breath, feel the bliss,
In the twilight's tender kiss.
Time slows down to let us be,
As stars awaken, wild and free.

The Drift of Celestial Threads

Woven dreams on velvet skies,
Where the cosmos softly lies.
Galaxies twirl, a dance of fate,
Guiding us to seek, not wait.

Nebulas bloom in colors bright,
Crafting tales in the silent night.
Every thread a story spun,
Uniting worlds, all as one.

Through the vastness, we will roam,
In the universe, we find home.
Navigating through the stars,
Chasing hopes, breaking bars.

As comets streak with fiery grace,
We embrace the endless space.
With every wish, a thread we weave,
In the drift of dreams, believe.

A Palette of Evolving Heavens

Brushstrokes of the sunset's glow,
Crafting wonders we don't know.
Colors merge in a soft dance,
Painting life's fleeting chance.

Clouds become a canvas wide,
With the breeze, they twist and glide.
Each hue tells a tale untold,
As day turns into night's fold.

The stars come out, a sparkling show,
In the dark, their beauty grows.
Shadows shift, revealing light,
In the palette of the night.

With every dawn, new shades arise,
A cycle painted in the skies.
Embrace the change, let colors sing,
In each moment, find the spring.

Comets in the Wake

In the silver night sky, they soar,
Trailing dreams of days long gone.
Whispers of light ignite the dark,
Chasing shadows, they dance on.

Bright tails of mysteries untold,
They paint the heavens with their glide.
Ephemeral, they spark a fire,
Leaving us in wonder, wide-eyed.

Time bends as they swiftly pass,
Carving tales on celestial seas.
Fleeting moments, a cosmic dash,
Reminders of life's swift decrees.

In quiet awe, we gaze in flight,
Caught in the beauty of their wake.
With each glimpse of their fleeting light,
We yearn for dreams that fate may take.

When the World Bends

In twilight's grasp, the world will sway,
Branches bending, roots hold tight.
Underneath the vast stars' play,
Shadows stretch in the pull of night.

The horizon whispers soft and low,
Secrets held in the moon's embrace.
Time twists gently, rivers flow,
As currents shift in a timeless race.

Through the bends, we seek the truth,
In the chaos, wisdom gleams.
Fragments of forgotten youth,
Revealed in dawn's first golden beams.

When the world bends, hearts entwined,
A melody plays in a bittersweet tune.
In this moment, we find what's blind,
United under a watchful moon.

Horizons Beyond Reach

Veils of mist hide distant shores,
Where dreams linger and yearn to be.
Silent calls from beyond the doors,
Whispers of what we wish to see.

Each step forward feels like a dance,
Towards horizons forever bright.
In every glance, we take a chance,
To discover what lies in the light.

Time unwinds and the journey weaves,
Through valleys deep and mountains high.
In every heartbeat, a hope believes,
That tomorrow holds another sky.

Yet, even when new worlds unfold,
Our souls remember the paths we crossed.
In the tapestry of tales retold,
We find strength in what never was lost.

Mirage of the Unreachable

Across the sands, a figure glows,
Dancing lightly in the heat.
With each step, the illusion grows,
A mirage of dreams we dare to meet.

The desert winds whisper abstract lore,
Promises woven in sunlight's thread.
Chasing shadows, we seek for more,
In the ether of what lies ahead.

Yet every glimmer fades away,
A fleeting ghost in the weary sun.
We learn to embrace the truth we play,
In every chase, we find we've won.

For in each heartbeat, there's a spark,
A light that guides us through the haze.
Though unreachable may seem the arc,
It's in the journey that our hearts blaze.

Flights of Fancy

In dreams we soar on wings so bright,
Through fields of stars in the quiet night.
With whispers soft from moonlit dreams,
We chase the glow of endless gleams.

In colors spun from hopes and sighs,
We paint our wishes across the skies.
Each flutter stirs a daring thought,
In realms of magic, we're freely caught.

Through currents strong, our spirits glide,
Where imagination takes the ride.
With every breath, we're free to roam,
In flights of fancy, we've found a home.

The Morphing Tides

The ocean breathes a tale anew,
With every wave that breaks in two.
Whispers of change in salted air,
As tides of life shape everywhere.

Moonlit pull and their sway divine,
The dance of water, a rhythmic line.
Each swell brings secrets, old and deep,
In rolling waves, our thoughts do leap.

From shore to sea, a shifting frame,
In nature's hands, we feel the same.
As shifting sands tell stories bold,
The morphing tides of life unfold.

Faded Echoes of the Day

The sun bows low, a gentle fade,
In shadows deep, the memories lade.
Soft hues linger, a whisper soft,
As twilight greets the stars aloft.

Faded echoes of laughter sweet,
In twilight's glow, our hearts do meet.
The day retreats, yet still we hold,
The warmth of moments long retold.

In evening's hush, a sigh, a pause,
As time slips by without a cause.
Yet in the night, dreams start to play,
In faded echoes of the day.

A Journey Beyond the Clouds

To skies aboard a hopeful dream,
Where wonders float and starlight beams.
Each cloud a wing, we rise and soar,
A journey paved to realms of yore.

With every gust, our spirits climb,
In sunlit paths of endless rhyme.
Through airy castles and breezy plains,
We chase the wild where freedom reigns.

Beyond the mist, where daylight spills,
A world awakens with gentle thrills.
In hushed delight, we dance and glide,
On journeys bright, our hearts abide.

The Showers of Transformation

In the morning light, they fall,
Gentle whispers, nature's call.
Seeds of change birthed from the sky,
Awakening the dreams that lie.

Colors blend in vibrant streams,
Washing away forgotten themes.
Each droplet shifts the weary ground,
A symphony of life profound.

The earth drinks deep, a hearty sigh,
While rains above begin to cry.
In every corner, new life grows,
From the depths where hope still flows.

Underneath the greyest hue,
Miracles are born anew.
In the shadows, change is near,
With showers bright, it becomes clear.

Shadows of the Celestial Sea

Stars like whispers, softly glow,
Reflecting secrets in the flow.
Beneath the dark, a tale is spun,
A sea of shadows, dreams begun.

Waves of twilight, gently crest,
Hidden insights, in the jest.
The night unfolds its velvet hue,
Crafting worlds where few wander through.

Crickets chirp their lullabies,
Under watchful, starlit skies.
Each moment drifts in silent plea,
In the depths of the celestial sea.

Guided by the moon's soft gaze,
We navigate the cosmic maze.
In shadows deep, the light will be,
A guiding force, setting us free.

Dances of Dimming Radiance

Fading twilight, color bows,
A graceful end where daylight sows.
Softly dims the evening's heat,
As dusk arrives on weary feet.

Whispers spin in gentle breeze,
Chasing echoes through the trees.
A dance of shadows, slow and low,
Welcomes night with a quiet glow.

The last of light, a fleeting sigh,
As stars awaken in the sky.
Each step a memory, bittersweet,
In silence, the heart finds its beat.

Listen close, the night will sing,
Of moments lost, yet held as offerings.
In dimming radiance, hope's embrace,
A myriad of dreams find their place.

Beyond the Shimmering Fractals

Patterns gleam in vibrant hue,
A cosmos born from shades anew.
Fractals dance in endless flight,
Revealing truths hidden from sight.

Each twist and turn, a tale unfolds,
Whispers of the brave and bold.
Beyond the shimmer, time extends,
Where the journey never ends.

Like rivers flowing, thoughts entwine,
In fractal worlds, paths align.
A tapestry woven, vast and grand,
In every corner, a guiding hand.

Embrace the chaos, learn to see,
Beauty lies in complexity.
Beyond the fractals, hearts can soar,
To realms of wonder, forevermore.

Refractions of Existence

In shadows deep, we find our way,
Fragments of light guide us each day.
Through mirrors bright, our truths unwind,
In every reflection, a story assigned.

Every moment a flicker, a chance,
Caught in the dance of a timeless expanse.
Life's colors blend in our hearts' embrace,
A spectrum of dreams in a fleeting space.

In whispers soft, the echoes call,
Each step we take, we rise or fall.
Through prisms of choice, our paths diverge,
In the fluid world, we constantly merge.

Refractions of life, a fragile art,
In every break, we play our part.
Together we flow, in currents we trust,
To paint our existence in colors robust.

A Wisp of Change

A gentle breeze stirs the calm sea,
Carrying whispers, wild and free.
In the quiet dawn, the shadows fade,
A wisp of change in the glen is laid.

Leaves rustle softly in the trees,
Speaking of journeys on the breeze.
With every shift in the morning light,
Old paths dissolve, new dreams ignite.

Moments of stillness before the storm,
Life's tapestry woven, a new form.
In fleeting glances, possibilities bloom,
From the ashes of doubt, we find our room.

With every heartbeat, we yearn to grow,
To dance with the tide, to bend, to flow.
Change wraps around us, gentle and wise,
In every ending, a new sunrise.

Veiled Horizons

Towards the distance, the horizon gleams,
Wrapped in the fabric of unspoken dreams.
Mist blankets valleys where secrets lay,
Veiled horizons beckon, leading the way.

Mountains stand tall, guardians of time,
Whispers of wisdom, echoing rhyme.
Within their shadows, the ancient dwell,
Each stone a story, each tale a spell.

Across the canvas of sky and earth,
Weaving our journeys, we question our worth.
In the twilight's embrace, hope begins,
As veils lift softly, new light seeps in.

With courage deep, let visions arise,
To pierce the fog with our daring eyes.
For beyond the veil, the truth may lie,
In veiled horizons, we learn to fly.

The Wings of Transition

In the cocoon, stillness resides,
Waiting for change, as time abides.
With the dawn break, a longing grows,
The wings of transition whisper soft flows.

Emerging slowly from shadows deep,
In tender moments, new dreams we reap.
A metamorphosis, profound and grand,
Learning to soar, leaving the land.

With fluttering hearts, we rise above,
Casting aside fear, embracing love.
Each wing is a promise, a tale to tell,
In the winds of change, we find our spell.

So let us fly through the skies unknown,
With the wings of transition, we have grown.
In every journey, we find our song,
A symphony of change where we all belong.

Manifestations at Dusk

Shadows dance on twilight's edge,
Whispers of dreams begin to surge.
Colors blend in fading light,
Secrets stir, igniting the night.

Echoes of wishes on the breeze,
In the stillness, hearts find ease.
Fleeting moments softly glide,
Wrapped in dusk, where hopes reside.

Murmurs of fate in twilight's glow,
Promises sworn in twilight's flow.
As stars awaken, stories bloom,
Manifested dreams dispel the gloom.

A canvas stretched, the world unfolds,
In hushed tones, our fate extols.
With every heartbeat, we embrace,
The magic born in dusk's embrace.

Map of the Unseen Path

Winding trails through forest deep,
Echoes of journeys, secrets we keep.
Each step taken, a choice unfolds,
A tale of courage waiting to be told.

Beneath the stars, we chart our course,
Navigating life with unseen force.
With every fork, new paths arise,
Guided by whispers, under vast skies.

Footprints etched in sands of time,
Every heartbeat, a rhythm, a rhyme.
Lost and found in the wild embrace,
The dance of fate, our sacred space.

With each turn, we learn and grow,
The map unwritten, yet we know.
In stillness, we find our way,
On the unseen path, come what may.

When Time Spills Over

Moments drip like melting wax,
Fleeting hours, a bittersweet ax.
Caught in laughter, caught in tears,
Time spills over, igniting our fears.

The clock ticks softly, yet so loud,
In every heartbeat, we're enshrouded.
Seasons change, but love remains,
In the flow of time, joy and pains.

As shadows stretch and daylight wanes,
Whispers linger, time reclaims.
Memories swirl, a treasurable art,
When time spills over, we share our heart.

Embrace the moments, hold them near,
In the spaces where we disappear.
Each tick a dance, each tock a song,
When time spills over, we belong.

The Timekeeper's Canvas

Brush strokes of moments paint the scene,
In every corner, visions glean.
Layers of time in colors bright,
The timekeeper's canvas, pure delight.

Each second captured, a story shown,
Fragments of life in hues alone.
From dawn's soft blush to twilight's sighs,
Artistry blooms as the old world dies.

With every tick, possibilities swell,
In the art of time, we weave our spell.
Capturing dreams in a fleeting glance,
On this canvas, we take our chance.

So let us paint with fervent strokes,
Create a world, drown out the hoax.
For the timekeeper's canvas, bold and vast,
Is a testament to futures cast.

Whispers of the Clouded Dawn

Morning breaks with muted light,
Shadows play in gentle flight.
Whispers linger, soft and low,
As the night begins to go.

Birds awaken, stretch their wings,
Nature hums and softly sings.
Clouds caress the waking sky,
In this moment, dreams can fly.

Raindrops dance on blushing leaves,
The world breathes in, then believes.
Colors shimmer, fade, and twirl,
In the dawn, life starts to whirl.

Silence breaks with whispers clear,
In the dawn, we're gathered near.
Every heartbeat, every sound,
In the magic, we are found.

Celestial Currents

Stars align in silent grace,
Twinkling lights in endless space.
Galaxies spin, a timeless dance,
In the night, we find romance.

Comets streak, like whispers bright,
Chasing dreams through velvet night.
Winds of space, a cosmic flow,
Draws our hearts where wonders grow.

Nebulas bloom in shades of blue,
Painting skies in every hue.
In the tapestry of time,
We are threads in a grand rhyme.

Infinite paths, we weave and roam,
In the cosmos, we find home.
Chasing echoes, we entwine,
In celestial currents, we align.

A Dusk in Transition

Golden rays begin to fade,
Painting dusk, a vibrant shade.
Whispers of the day retreat,
As the night takes up the seat.

Crickets chirp their evening song,
In the twilight, we belong.
Shadows stretch, and moonlight glows,
In the hush, serenity flows.

Branches sway in tender breeze,
Rustling leaves of swaying trees.
Colors blend, a canvas bright,
As the day surrenders light.

Stars emerge from velvet cloak,
Each one spins a timeless joke.
In this pause, we hold our breath,
A dance between the dusk and death.

Tides of the Horizon

Waves caress the sandy shore,
Whispers of the ocean's roar.
Tidal pull, a rhythmic sway,
Guides us gently, come what may.

Sunset paints the waters gold,
Stories of the sea retold.
Distant ships in silhouette,
Dreams upon the waves are set.

Seagulls soar on currents free,
Tracing arcs across the sea.
In the twilight, hearts unite,
In the glow of fading light.

As the tide begins to change,
Moments shift, our lives arrange.
With each wave, we learn to flow,
In the tides of life, we grow.

Moondust and Sunlight

In a quiet night sky, stars gleam bright,
Whispers of dreams in soft silver light.
Moondust dances on shadows so deep,
Awakening secrets that night tends to keep.

Sunlight peeks through the dawn's tender veil,
Warming the world like a heart's gentle sail.
Nature awakens, the day comes alive,
In the embrace of warmth, spirits thrive.

Fleeting Moments Tethered

Time flows like water, swift and serene,
Holding on tight to moments unseen.
Each laugh, each tear, a thread finely spun,
A tapestry woven in light of the sun.

Fleeting moments like whispers in air,
Captured in memories, precious and rare.
Tethered together by love's gentle grace,
In the dance of existence, we find our place.

The Ethereal Whisper

In twilight's embrace, silence descends,
An ethereal whisper, the heart transcends.
Words left unspoken, yet felt in the air,
A connection so deep, it lingers somewhere.

Echoes of longing in shadows will sway,
Guiding the souls that have wandered astray.
Through the stillness, a promise so sweet,
An unbroken bond where two pathways meet.

Kaleidoscope of Fate

Stars collide in a cosmic play,
A kaleidoscope of fate leads the way.
Colors entwined in a vibrant embrace,
Destinies shift, time quickens its pace.

Every choice a brushstroke, bold and bright,
Creating a canvas of day and night.
In the swirl of existence, dreams intertwine,
In the dance of our lives, we forever shine.

Tapestry of the Heavens

Stars weave dreams in the night,
Whispers of light take flight.
Galaxies dance, a cosmic play,
Painting wishes in the sway.

Nebulas burst in vibrant hue,
Silent songs of the astral view.
Constellations sing of old,
Stories of the brave and bold.

Planets spin in gentle grace,
Each a guardian of its place.
Comets streak with tales untold,
Eternal journeys, bright and bold.

In the darkness, hope ignites,
The tapestry unfolds in sights.
A universe of endless streams,
Binding together all our dreams.

Fluctuations of Light

A flicker here, a shimmer there,
Moments caught in gentle air.
Light darts playfully around,
A dance of shadows, softly found.

Reflections weave a golden thread,
Illuminating paths we tread.
Every glimmer tells a tale,
A fleeting vision riding the gale.

Through the prism, colors burst,
In every hue, a quiet thirst.
Fluctuations shift and sway,
Guiding us through night and day.

In this realm of bright embrace,
We find our joy, our sacred space.
Each ray a whisper, tender and bright,
A world alive in the play of light.

Genesis of a New Dawn

Awakening in soft repose,
Morning's light begins to rose.
Whispers of a brand new day,
Promises in golden ray.

Horizon blushes, shades ignite,
Chasing shadows from the night.
With each breath, a chance to grow,
Seeds of hope in winds that blow.

Birds take flight, their songs resound,
Nature's chorus all around.
Life emerges, fresh and bright,
A canvas painted in pure light.

In the stillness, dreams take form,
Embracing warmth, weathering storm.
This genesis, a sacred vow,
To rise again, to live, not bow.

The Art of Temporary

Moments pass like grains of sand,
Fleeting echoes, we understand.
In laughter's breath, in sorrow's sigh,
Life's a canvas, colors fly.

Each heartbeat breathes a different tune,
Underneath the waning moon.
Joy and pain, a dance so sweet,
Every ending makes us complete.

Chasing sunsets, dreams unfold,
Stories written, quietly told.
The art of living day by day,
Finding beauty in the gray.

Though all we know may slip away,
Memories linger, softly stay.
In this transient, wondrous spree,
We find the art in being free.

Remnants of a Vanishing Light

In twilight's embrace, shadows dance slow,
Where whispers of yesteryear softly flow.
Fading echoes trace the contours of night,
Leaving us with remnants of once burning bright.

Once fierce and bold, the candles now dim,
Hearts flicker gently, on memories we skim.
The canvas of dreams wears a tattered thread,
Yet hope lingers softly, where fears once led.

The Ballet of the Wind

The wind pirouettes through the swaying trees,
A dancer of nature, alluring with ease.
It tumbles and twirls, a soft serenade,
Whispering secrets in the twilight's shade.

With each graceful move, it stirs the air,
Carving paths through silence with a gentle flair.
It carries our dreams on its silken shawl,
A symphony shared, uniting us all.

Echoes of Celestial Journeys

Stars weave their tales in the fabric of night,
Navigating dark, they shimmer and light.
Galaxies dance in an endless embrace,
A cosmic ballet through vastness and space.

Each echo a story, each light a deep sigh,
Reminds us we're part of the endless sky.
In whispers of stardust, our dreams intertwine,
As we journey to places where worlds align.

Migrations of the Ether

Waves of the ether, they pulse and they flow,
Carrying whispers where soft breezes blow.
Travellers drift on unseen currents wide,
In a dance with the cosmos, they gracefully glide.

With each fleeting moment, they weave through our days,

Guiding our thoughts in mysterious ways.
They sing of the past and the futures untold,
In the tapestry woven, both daring and bold.

Flight of Gossamer Dreams

Wings of silk stretch wide and far,
Chasing whispers of a distant star.
On a breeze, my spirit glides,
Where the heart and hope collide.

Clouds embrace like tender arms,
Cradling secrets, holding charms.
In the twilight's gentle sigh,
I lose my fears, I learn to fly.

Dancing lightly on the air,
With each moment, free of care.
Gossamer threads weave through my dreams,
Nurtured by the moonlight beams.

As horizons blur and fade,
In this dreamscape, I'm remade.
Ethereal paths, I shall chase,
In the warmth of dream's embrace.

Between Daylight and Nightfall

The sun dips low, a golden hue,
While shadows stretch and blend with blue.
Whispers of dusk, soft and clear,
Signal the night will soon appear.

In this space, magic unfolds,
Stories of both young and old.
Stars awake in twilight's grasp,
Each glimmering light, a dream to clasp.

Colors merge, a painted sky,
As day bids night a soft goodbye.
Hints of lavender and deep maroon,
Echo the song of a gentle tune.

Between the moments, still I stand,
In the beauty of a fleeting land.
Each heartbeat pulses, time does bend,
In the embrace of night's soft end.

A Skyward Reverie

Gazing up where the eagles soar,
In quest of dreams I can't ignore.
The vastness calls, the winds invite,
To dance with stars and seek the light.

Clouds like ships on a sea of blue,
Charting courses, old and new.
In a realm where wishes rise,
I chase the secrets held in skies.

Pastel hues in the dawn's embrace,
Whispers of hope in this sacred space.
Every sigh of the wind's sweet song,
Soothes my spirit, bids me strong.

As daylight breaks, I softly muse,
Catching dreams I cannot lose.
Upward still, my heart will roam,
In a skyward reverie, I find home.

The Palette of Infinity

A canvas spread, a world untamed,
Brushstrokes wild, colors unnamed.
Each hue a tale of joy and pain,
In the vastness where dreams remain.

Waves of blue, the depths of night,
Crimson flames, a heart's delight.
Golden rays that kiss the dawn,
In this palette, life is drawn.

Every shade holds memories dear,
From laughter shared to silent tears.
With each stroke, I create my fate,
In the theater of dreams, I wait.

Brush and heart working in sync,
Painting visions, on the brink.
The palette swells, infinity calls,
In this masterpiece, my spirit sprawls.

Radiance in the Flux of Time

In the gentle ebb of day,
Moments weave like gentle streams,
Flickering memories remain,
Shimmering in our quiet dreams.

Time, a river softly flows,
Carrying whispers of the past,
Each second like a blooming rose,
In the garden where we cast.

Ephemeral, like morning dew,
A touch of gold on every face,
With every breath, a world anew,
In this fleeting, sacred space.

Radiance dances in the night,
Filling hearts with timeless light,
Through the shadows, we will glide,
In the flux, our souls abide.

Serenade of the Fading Horizon

As day surrenders to the night,
Fingers trace the sky's embrace,
Whispers soft and void of fright,
Painting dreams in twilight's space.

The stars emerge, a tender song,
Serenading with silver gleams,
In the stillness, we belong,
Caught within this weave of dreams.

Horizons blur in hues of gold,
Far and wide where hearts unite,
Stories of the brave and bold,
Breathe alive in gentle light.

With every dusk, a new ballet,
A dance of colors fades away,
Yet in this fleeting, soft repose,
Love's serenade forever grows.

Whispers of the Celestial Dance

Underneath the velvet dome,
Stars twinkle in a cosmic trance,
Each heartbeat finds its rightful home,
In the whispers of the dance.

Galaxies twirl, oh so bright,
Eclipsing shadows in their wake,
In the silence of the night,
We gather dreams that never break.

Orbs of light in harmony,
Guide the lost with radiant grace,
In the vast infinity,
We embrace this timeless space.

Dancing freely through the air,
Spirits soar without a care,
In this celestial embrace,
We find our place, our sacred space.

Colors of the Dusk and Dawn

When dusk unveils its canvas deep,
Brushstrokes of crimson, gold, and blue,
As daylight gives its gentle sweep,
The world awakes in colors new.

Eclipsing shadows come to play,
With whispers soft, the night will fall,
Yet dawn will chase the dark away,
In the light, we hear the call.

Each hue a promise softly gleamed,
From amber skies to violet plains,
In every shade, a dream redeemed,
Life's palette swirls with love's refrains.

Colors dance in sweet embrace,
Fleeting moments, time's sweet brush,
Together we shall find our place,
In the dusk and dawn's soft hush.

Cadence of the Elements

Water whispers secrets soft,
Earth holds stories deep and oft.
Fire ignites with passion's flare,
Air sings freedom, light as air.

Each element a dance divine,
Together crafting form and line.
In nature's grip, they swirl and blend,
A cycle that will never end.

Harmonies in Flux

Waves crash upon the sandy shore,
Melodies of nature evermore.
Clouds drift slowly in the sky,
Echoes of a lullaby.

Leaves rustle as the breezes sigh,
At twilight's cusp, colors comply.
In the dance of change we find,
A symphony of heart and mind.

The Lattice of Becoming

Threads of fate intertwine and weave,
In each moment, we believe.
Shadows blend with light's embrace,
Transforming time, an endless chase.

Forms uncoil, then stretch anew,
Patterns shifting into view.
In every turn, a chance to grow,
A lattice built on what we sow.

Dance of the Celestial Spheres

Stars align in cosmic grace,
Planets spin in endless race.
Moons reflect the sun's bright glow,
Galaxies in ebb and flow.

In the night, a ballet bright,
Orbits drawing paths of light.
The dance unfolds, a grand display,
Guiding hearts along their way.

Epilogues of Enchantment

In twilight's glow, whispers align,
Fading dreams on the edge of time.
Stars awaken, the night is young,
Magic stitches songs unsung.

Beneath the moon's soft embrace,
Stories linger in every space.
A tapestry of love unfolds,
In the silence, truth beholds.

Winds carry secrets from afar,
Guiding hearts beneath a star.
With every sigh, enchantment breathes,
Life's fragile thread, the heart believes.

In shadowy glades where echoes play,
Whispers of fate lead us away.
Through darkened woods, we find our way,
In the beauty of night, we choose to stay.

Imagining Tomorrow's Sky

Painted horizons in shades of gold,
Dreams take flight, brave and bold.
Clouds drift softly, a canvas wide,
In the heart of hope, we take our stride.

Whispers of dawn, a gentle tune,
Promises bloom beneath the moon.
With every heartbeat, futures grow,
In the cradle of night, stars aglow.

Together we chase the morning light,
Hand in hand, destined for flight.
As shadows fade and daylight wakes,
Through the unknown, our journey takes.

With every dream, new paths to find,
Tomorrow's sky forever kind.
In the dance of life, we learn to soar,
Opening wings, seeking more.

The Fractured Light

Shattered fragments across the floor,
Echoes of laughter, forevermore.
In broken glass, reflections gleam,
Whispers of hope in a waking dream.

Through the cracks, a radiance seeps,
Memories linger, where silence keeps.
In the fading glow, shadows play,
Colorful dusk gives night its sway.

Beneath the surface, a fire burns,
With every heartache, a lesson learned.
In fractured sights, we find our way,
Guided by fragments, night and day.

From chaos rises a silent song,
In the seams of life, we all belong.
Through shattered light, we stand as one,
In the web of fate, the battle won.

Stillness Between Storms

In the hush before the rain,
Nature breathes, a sweet refrain.
Clouds gather with a silent might,
Yet here we stand, in calm twilight.

Whispers of trees sway gently near,
The world holds its breath, filled with fear.
Yet in this pause, peace flows free,
A fragile moment, just you and me.

As thunder rumbles in the skies,
We find comfort in quiet sighs.
Between the chaos, love ignites,
In the stillness, our hearts take flight.

Through storms we weather, hand in hand,
Together we stand, together we stand.
In the eye of the tempest, our spirits thrive,
In the stillness, we feel alive.

The Lullaby of Shifting Hues

In twilight's glow, the colors blend,
Whispers soft as day meets night.
Each shade unfolds, a gentle hand,
Cradling dreams in muted light.

The stars emerge, a tender kiss,
Painting hopes with silken threads.
In this embrace, we find our bliss,
Night's symphony softly spreads.

The dawn will chase the night away,
Yet still we hold the twilight sweet.
Each hue a promise, come what may,
In this lullaby, our hearts meet.

With every breath, we sway and drift,
In nature's arms, we find our way.
The colors shift, a perfect gift,
In this dance of night and day.

Glimpse Beyond the Veil

In shadows cloaked, the secrets lie,
A world unseen yet close at hand.
With open hearts, we dare to fly,
To where the mysteries expand.

Through fragile threads of twilight mist,
We glimpse the fabric of our dreams.
A dance of fate, a lover's tryst,
Where nothing's ever as it seems.

The veil may part, the light may shine,
With every step, we find our place.
In whispered truth, our spirits twine,
And trust unveils the hidden grace.

In every breath, a story spun,
A tapestry with threads so fine.
Beyond the veil, we're all as one,
Eternal echoes, love's design.

Horizons Reimagined

The sun dips low, a canvas bright,
Where dreams and wishes take their flight.
With every dawn, we write anew,
Our hearts alight with vibrant hue.

Mountains rise and valleys sigh,
Revealing paths where hopes can fly.
In every step, the world expands,
A future painted by our hands.

With each horizon, stories bloom,
On paths untraveled, dispel the gloom.
Adventure calls, an open door,
To seek the wonders, evermore.

Together we will chase the light,
With courage strong, we'll take our flight.
Horizons wait, a call to roam,
In every heart, we find our home.

The Flicker of Possibilities

A spark ignites, a flicker bright,
In shadows deep, the dreams take flight.
With every pulse, the magic grows,
In whispered thoughts, the future glows.

Infinite paths, a choice to make,
Each step unveiled, for courage's sake.
Embrace the fire, let visions soar,
In endless realms, forevermore.

The heart's desire knows no bounds,
In every moment, potential sounds.
From tiny sparks, great fires rise,
In every hope, the spirit flies.

A tapestry we weave in time,
With threads of fate, our dreams will climb.
In every flicker, life unfolds,
The stories waiting to be told.

In the Embrace of Changing Winds

The whispers dance through bending trees,
A melody of shifting leaves.
With every gust, a tale unfolds,
Of dreams that drift like autumn gold.

The sky, a canvas, swirling bright,
As day concedes to tender night.
In quietude, the heart finds grace,
Amidst the winds, a warm embrace.

Clouds gather close, a fleeting friend,
In their shadows, we descend.
Yet like the seasons, we embrace,
The changes etched on time's own face.

In every breath, the world does spin,
A dance of fate, where we begin.
With open arms, we face the skies,
In changing winds, our spirit flies.

Daybreak's Secret

A gentle light through curtains streams,
Awakens soft and fleeting dreams.
The world stirs under dawn's embrace,
As shadows fade, and time finds space.

Birds begin their morning song,
In melodies where hearts belong.
Each note a breath, a promise made,
In daybreak's warmth, our fears will fade.

The dew-kissed grass, a jeweled sight,
Reflects the whispers of the night.
In every glimmer, secrets shared,
In daybreak's glow, we find we dared.

As sun climbs high, the shadows flee,
Revealing paths to all we see.
In morning's light, our hopes ignite,
A fresh beginning, pure and bright.

Celestial Transitions

Stars flicker in the velvet night,
Each one a spark, a guiding light.
In cosmic dances, hearts unite,
As planets spin in graceful flight.

The moon ascends, a silver queen,
Casting dreams on the night's serene.
In whispers soft, the cosmos speaks,
Of hidden truths that soul seeks.

Each moment shifts, the universe,
In rhythms deep, a boundless verse.
With every heartbeat, time concedes,
Celestial transitions plant the seeds.

We drift on waves of stardust bright,
In every glance, a shared delight.
Across the skies, our spirits roam,
In cosmic dance, we find our home.

The Unraveling Canvas

Each thread a color, bold and bright,
Woven stories come to light.
The canvas stretches, wide and grand,
A tapestry crafted by gentle hand.

As brush meets surface, dreams take flight,
In strokes of passion, shadows fight.
Yet with each mark, a truth revealed,
In unraveling, our hearts are healed.

The colors clash, yet harmonize,
In chaos, beauty often lies.
With every tear, we learn to see,
The art of life, its mystery.

As layers lift, new views appear,
In life's great canvas, we draw near.
With open hearts, we paint our way,
In the unraveling, we find our sway.

Ephemeral Dreamscapes

In whispers soft, the shadows play,
Colors dance as night meets day.
Fleeting visions, lost in time,
Echoes fade, like muted chime.

Beneath a sky where stardust flows,
Reality blurs, and wonder grows.
Silken threads weave tales untold,
In this realm where dreams unfold.

A fleeting touch, a soft embrace,
Moments vanish, leave no trace.
Yet in our hearts, they still reside,
Ephemeral, yet they abide.

In quiet corners of the mind,
These dreamscapes, rare, we often find.
Gliding through, like feathers drift,
In twilight's glow, our spirits lift.

When Light Bends

When morning spills its golden hue,
The world awakens, bright and new.
Shadows stretch, as beams descend,
Embracing light, as day begins.

In silver streams, reflections twine,
Nature whispers, sweet and fine.
Moments captured in glimmers bright,
A canvas painted with pure light.

As twilight falls, the colors blend,
With every curve, the shadows bend.
Softly, dusk wraps dreams in grace,
In gentle folds, we find our place.

When light bends low and silence breathes,
The heart finds peace in what it sees.
A dance of hues, a fleeting art,
Each ray of light, a work of heart.

Veils of Twilight

Veils of twilight, softly drawn,
Curtains fall as day is gone.
A hush descends, the stars align,
In quiet whispers, worlds entwine.

Misty shadows weave their thread,
In twilight's glow, the dreams are fed.
As day kisses night, secrets swell,
In the stillness, magic dwells.

With every breath, a story weaves,
In silver light, the heart believes.
Through the veil, we glimpse the grace,
Of hidden realms where wishes trace.

In this embrace, we float and sway,
Through veils of twilight, we drift away.
Each moment born, to fade and bloom,
In the depth of night, dispelling gloom.

The Call of the Horizon

The horizon whispers, soft and low,
Promising paths where dreamers go.
A line that beckons, wide and deep,
In its embrace, our hopes we keep.

Where sky meets earth, the colors blend,
A journey waiting, around each bend.
With every step, the heart takes flight,
Chasing the dawn, embracing the night.

In golden rays, the future gleams,
The call of the horizon fuels our dreams.
With hands outstretched, we reach for more,
Like waves that kiss the distant shore.

For in that line, where time stands still,
Lies the promise of the unseen thrill.
So let us wander, unafraid to roam,
To find our place, to make it home.

Milton Keynes UK
Ingram Content Group UK Ltd.
UKHW022117251124
451529UK00012B/570